Guide to I
Pub

Charles and Jamie Wildgoose

COUNTRYSIDE BOOKS
NEWBURY BERKSHIRE

First published 2017
© Charles and Jamie Wildgoose 2017

COUNTRYSIDE BOOKS
3 Catherine Road
Newbury, Berkshire

To view our complete range of books,
please visit us at
www.countrysidebooks.co.uk

ISBN 978 1 84674 346 7

Cover design by Barrie Appleby

Designed by KT Designs, St Helens
Produced through The Letterworks Ltd., Reading
Typeset by KT Designs, St Helens
Printed in Poland

Introduction

Here are twenty of my father's walks in the Peak District. They have been taken from three early guides he wrote, now long out of print, and have been fully revised and updated. They are still packed with interest and offer wonderful things to see. There's Lud's Church (which legend says may have once been a hiding place for Robin Hood), the remains of a Roman fort, and Hob Hurst's House (an ancient burial site, named after an elf or goblin said to live in the nearby woods) – and I've not even mentioned the views yet.

Wear a pair of boots and plan for bad weather. It may be sunny when you set off, but you never know when things might take a turn – and it's often when you're as far from the car as you're going to be! You should also take a drink and a bite to eat with you, if you're walking a few miles and it gets hot it pays to keep a bottle of water close by.

Whilst it is possible to follow these walks by the sketch map and directions provided, it's also worth taking the appropriate OS map for the area you'll be walking in. That way, if you should stray off the path, you have an additional reference.

I would like to thank my testers – without whom this book would not have been possible – so thank you to Jim Bannister and Rosie Abbott, Angela & Chris Bush, Stuart, Fran & Coralie Rooker, and Anna Cole.

Very special thanks to my wife, Sophie – and of course my Dad, Charles Wildgoose.

Enjoy your walking.

Jamie Wildgoose

Publisher's Note

We hope that you obtain considerable enjoyment from this book; great care has been taken in its preparation. However, changes of landlord and actual pub closures are sadly not uncommon. Likewise, although at the time of publication all routes followed public rights of way or permitted paths, diversion orders can be made and permissions withdrawn.

We cannot, of course, be held responsible for such diversion orders and any inaccuracies in the text which result from these or any other changes to the routes, nor any damage which might result from walkers trespassing on private property. We are anxious though that all details covering the walks and the pubs are kept up to date and would therefore welcome information from readers which would be relevant to future editions.

The simple sketch maps that accompany the walks in this book are based on notes made by the author whilst checking out the routes on the ground. However, for the benefit of a proper map, we do recommend that you purchase the relevant Ordnance Survey sheet covering your walk.

To get in touch visit our website: www.countrysidebooks.co.uk

The Castle Hotel, Castleton

1 Dovestone Reservoir

2.5 or 4.3 miles (4 or 6.8 km)

WALK HIGHLIGHTS

The walk circumnavigates Dovestone Reservoir (built in the 1960s) and Yeoman Hey Reservoir (built in the 1880s) on a track for part of the way and on fairly reasonable paths for the rest – though there's one section that can be a bit uneven.

THE PUB

The Royal George www.facebook.com/royalgeorgesaddleworth
☎ 01457 837851 **OL3 7HX**

THE WALK

1 Walk to the south end of the car park and bear left up the steps to the dam. Then turn right to a tarmac access road 30 yards away, turning left along this. Pass the Dove Stone Sailing Club building on your left (you will often see 'Dove Stone' as an alternative form of 'Dovestone'). Ignore a farm entrance sharp right. Go through a gate and follow the public footpath along the track to the right of the boatyard. Pass the Life

5

Guide to Peak District Pub Walks

HOW TO GET THERE: Dovestone Reservoir is reached from the A635 between Mossley and Holmfirth. Approaching from Mossley, drive north-eastwards and ½ a mile beyond the Clarence in Greenfield fork right for the reservoir. **Postcode** OL3 7NE

HOW TO GET TO THE PUB: From the reservoir car park, return to the A635, then turn left for 2 miles – the Royal George is on your left on Manchester Road, Greenfield. **Postcode** OL3 7HX

MAP: OS Explorer OL1 The Peak District – Dark Peak area (GR 013036).

PARKING: In the car park at the reservoir. This can get very busy at weekends and holidays, so arrive early. There is additional parking at Binn Green, where a short footpath joins this walk around Point 3.

for a Life Memorial Garden on your left. Then cross Chew Brook by a fairly substantial bridge. Turn left immediately along a tarmac path. Pass another Life for a Life plantation, a memorial forest, on your left. Stay on the stony path with the reservoir to your left. After ½ mile you reach Ashway Gap, where there used to be a house (Ashway Gap House). Cross the footbridge, continuing on the stony path. You reach a point where you can bear left across the dam between Dovestone Reservoir and Yeoman Hey Reservoir. For the shorter walk, turn left here and pick up the route at point 3.

2 If you're doing the whole circuit, then bear right on the footpath (without crossing the dam). Stay on this for ½ a mile or so – this section is quite stony and uneven. Yeoman Hey Reservoir is to your left as you go. Beyond the end of Yeoman Hey Reservoir, fork left, ignoring a right fork uphill. The dam bank of Greenfield Reservoir should be above you. When you reach it, cross the bridge over a stream. Bear left on the track beyond. Where the track forks, take the right fork uphill. On reaching a gravel track turn left. Keep on this track until you come back to the banking between Dovestone Reservoir and Yeoman Hey Reservoir – after turning left, turn right almost immediately.

3 Stay in the direction you were heading in. After 50 yards turn left through a kissing gate beside a farm gate – it's signed 'Dove Stone Car Park'. This path leads you down towards the reservoir, with a plantation to your right. Continue for ½ a mile to reach the overflow.

4 Turn sharp left at the end of the fence to cross the banking to return to the car park.

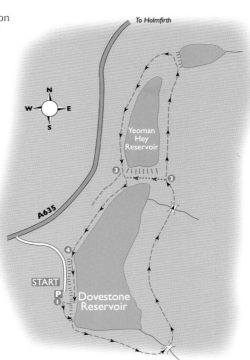

PLACES OF INTEREST NEARBY

Head north-west to Uppermill to have a look at the **Huddersfield Narrow Canal**. Here you'll find an inland waterway running just 20 miles which crosses the Pennines by means of 74 locks. Construction finished in 1811 but the canal was all but abandoned by 1944 due to easier and more profitable transport means. However, it has since been restored and it reopened to boats in 2001 and there's plenty to see.

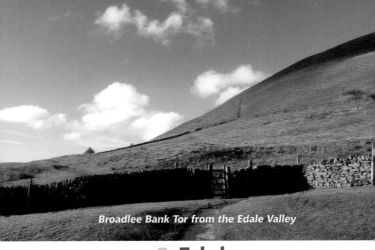

Broadlee Bank Tor from the Edale Valley

2 Edale
3.75 miles (6 km)

WALK HIGHLIGHTS
This walk covers the start of the Pennine Way but it isn't too strenuous if you pace yourself. All around there are marvellous views of the surrounding countryside including Mam Tor and Lose Hill. You'll descend into Upper Booth, 'booth' meaning very small village, and then onto Barber Booth. There's stunning Peak District scenery in every direction.

THE PUB
The Rambler Inn www.theramblerinn.com
☎ 01433 670268 **S33 7ZA**

THE WALK
① From the car park head out onto the road past the toilet block. Turn up the road past the Rambler Inn on your left. Then pass Fieldhead campsite and the visitor centre on your right. Keep on up the lane. Pass between the church and the old churchyard.

HOW TO GET THERE: Follow the Edale Road north from the A6187 at Hope. Stay on this for 5 miles to reach Edale's village centre. **Postcode** S33 7ZL

MAP: OS Explorer OL1 The Peak District – Dark Peak area (GR 013036).

PARKING: There is a pay and display car park on the right as you enter Edale.

2 At the Old Nags Head you've reached the start of the Pennine Way. Turn left a few yards before the pub on the path signed for 'Upper Booth and Pennine Way'. Pass through a gate almost immediately and walk uphill beside a small brook. After going through a small gate turn left, following the Pennine Way 'acorn' waymarks. Broadlee Bank Tor rises above you, and the Edale valley is to your left. Follow the obvious path through the fields for the next ¼ mile to reach a more open grassy area with a steep bank to your right. Keep straight forward along the Pennine Way

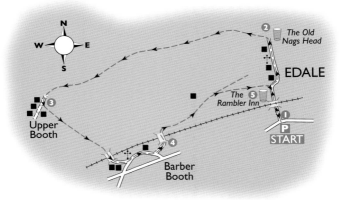

(and Jacob's Ladder) path, ignoring a right fork for Crowden Brook. Go through a small gate as a wide valley opens out before you. Follow the obvious path down. After going through a wicket gate the path begins to descend more directly towards the valley. Eventually the Pennine Way follows a track down towards Upper Booth, a small collection of properties. On reaching a stony track, turn left down it for 15 yards.

3 Pass through a wicket gate beside the farm gate on your left. In the first field head just to the left of Mam Nick (the 'nick' in the horizon ahead). In the second field head almost directly towards the Nick. Walk along the right side of fields three and four, before bearing slightly right in the fifth field to pass through a wicket gate. In the sixth field follow a grassy track, still aiming towards the Nick. Stay on this track now until it takes you alongside the railway, then over it at bridge 59. Stay on the track, walking directly through the farmyard (of Whitmore Lea Farm). Keep forward along a tarmac lane, ignoring a track forking right. Pass Edale Methodist chapel on your left to come out onto a narrow lane in Barber Booth.

4 Turn left. Immediately beyond Brookfield, bear left up a track for Grindsbrook Booth and Edale station. Cross bridge 58. Pass through a small gate on your right just beyond and follow the path along the left side of the narrow field. Keep on the bottom side of the second field, continuing across the third field and along the bottom side of the fourth. In the next field (with a farm at the top) bear slightly left to the wicket gate opposite. Cross the bridge and farm track beyond and head for the stile 30 yards away. In the field beyond, walk alongside the fence on your right for 10 yards - keep along this line (ignoring a stile which is a quarter left of you) to cross a stile. Then walk along the left side of the fields ahead to reach the road.

5 Turn right down the road back to the Rambler Inn and the car park.

PLACES OF INTEREST NEARBY
The Chestnut Centre Otter, Owl and Wildlife Park in Chapel-en-le-Frith, is a conservation park set in rolling countryside, and is home to many rare birds and mammals. www.chestnutcentre.co.uk

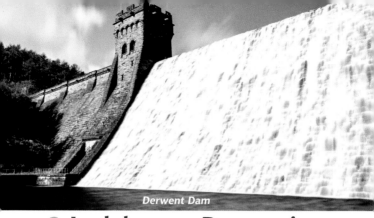
Derwent Dam

3 Ladybower Reservoir
5.8 miles (9.3 km)

WALK HIGHLIGHTS
This is a very level walk around Ladybower Reservoir, with no climbs to speak of, giving you a chance to enjoy the delightful Peakland scenery from below. Although the route might seem a bit obvious, the things you see on it will leave you well rewarded. Soon after you leave the car park go and have a look at the size of the stones in the dam wall of Derwent Reservoir, which was constructed between 1901 and 1916.

THE PUB
The Yorkshire Bridge Inn www.yorkshire-bridge.co.uk
☎ 01433 651361 **S33 0AZ**

THE WALK
From the Visitor Centre in the car park, follow the path signed 'To Dams'. On reaching the tarmac lane turn right. Head towards the wall of Derwent Reservoir. Follow the road as it bears right and rises steadily. Ignore the sharp left turn – a bridleway leading to Slippery Stones.

Pass Old House Farm on your left. Then pass the old schoolhouse (now St

11

Guide to Peak District Pub Walks

HOW TO GET THERE: Turn off the A57 Snake Road just west of the point where it is joined by the A6013 at Ladybower. Drive northwards beside the reservoir, signposted 'Derwent Valley'. This dead-end road reaches the Fairholmes car park after 2½ miles. **Postcode** S33 0AQ

HOW TO GET TO THE PUB: To get to the Yorkshire Bridge Inn from the reservoir, return to the A57, turn left and then go right at the traffic lights onto the A6013. The inn is on the right after ¾ of a mile. **Postcode** S33 0AZ

MAP: OS Explorer OL1 The Peak District – Dark Peak area.

PARKING: The Fairholmes car park. This popular car park can be very busy at weekends and bank holidays so try to get there early if you can!

Henry's). Ignore a footpath forking left, to stay on the lane as it descends and bears left, then right around an 'inlet'. The tarmac track is now more of a stony one. Pass the path on your left signed 'Via Derwent Edge for Moscar'. Stay on this track, still with the reservoir on your right. A mile or so later you reach a tarmac road beyond a gate; bear right down to the A57.

3 Turn sharp right over Ashopton Viaduct, and 400 yards later turn right again. Then, almost immediately, take the concessionary footpath for Fairholmes. The views are even better on this side of the reservoir. Stay on the obvious path with the reservoir still on your right. Pass a valve house to your left – water can be diverted into another pipe here if repairs are necessary. Your path then forks right off the grassy track you've been following. As you go, the path literally runs between the 5ft-high pipes of the Derwent Valley aqueduct.

4 You then walk very near the road on your left, but the path soon bears away from it. Eventually, ½ a mile later, the path brings you back to the road, by a car park.

5 Turn right here to get back to the Fairholmes car park.

PLACES OF INTEREST NEARBY

Explore the **Derwent** and **Howden dams** further up the valley. These were made famous by the dambusters who used them for practice runs during the Second World War. You may also see the memorial to 'Tip', a sheepdog who stayed with the body of his owner, in the snow, for 15 weeks between December and March in the early 1950s – we don't get winters like that nowadays.

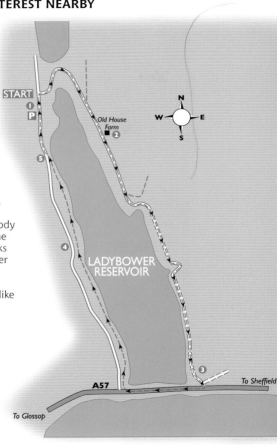

13

4 Redmires Reservoirs

2 miles (3.2 km)

WALK HIGHLIGHTS

A steady amble through delightful countryside. Starting off alongside the Upper Reservoir, you'll soon be walking at the side of a conduit as you get out onto the moorland. Redmires Upper Reservoir was completed in the mid 19th century and holds 300 million gallons of water. The reservoirs were built to provide clean drinking water via a water course following a cholera epidemic in 1832.

THE PUB

The Three Merry Lads www.thethreemerrylads.co.uk
☎ 0114 2302824 **S10 4LJ**

THE WALK

1 Turn left from the car park along the track with the reservoir on your right. After 400 yards, at the end of the reservoir, turn left along the footpath running beside the conduit on your left. This is an easy access track that takes you for nearly a mile to a crossing path. As you go, to the right there are good views across to the western outskirts of Sheffield.

2 On reaching a bridge (and with a footpath to your right on to the moorland and open access land in front of you), turn left over the bridge

HOW TO GET THERE: Follow Ringinglow Road westward from the A625 in Sheffield. At Ringinglow take the right turn. After that keep left at each road junction to reach the Redmires Reservoirs. **Postcode** S10 4LJ

HOW TO GET TO THE PUB: To get to the Three Merry Lads, turn left out of the car park and keep on Redmires Road until you reach the pub on your left. **Postcode** S10 4LJ

MAP: OS Explorer OL1 The Peak District – Dark Peak area (GR 256856).

PARKING: There is a car park beside the most westerly of the three reservoirs. It's on the right just before a left-hand bend – don't park at the first car park you reach on your right.

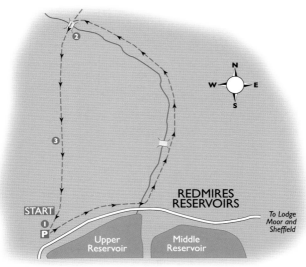

and follow the grassy track rising gently through the heather. This runs alongside a ruined wall on your right, though after 200 yards it bears slightly left away from it. Now you should be aiming for a wall some 200 yards ahead. On reaching this wall walk up the banking in front of you, with the wall to your left. At the top of the banking the path levels out. Continue beside the wall until you reach a boggy area in a valley.

3 Cross this via the duck-boarding and rise up the valley side ahead – keeping the wall on your left. Continue beside this until you get back to the car park. As you go you will get a good view of all three reservoirs in the valley.

PLACES OF INTEREST NEARBY

The **Botanical Gardens** in Sheffield offer 'stunning collections of trees and shrubs set in a historic landscape created in 1836'. They are near to the Royal Hallamshire Hospital, a mile south-west of the city centre. www.sbg.org.uk

The village of Hope with Lose Hill on the left and Win Hill on the right

5 Hope
3 miles (4.8 km)

WALK HIGHLIGHTS

One mile to the north of Hope lie Win Hill and Lose (pronounced "Loose") Hill. It's believed that over 1,000 years ago a battle was fought here with the winners camping on Win Hill and the losers ... yes, you've got it. The walk takes you directly over all that remains of the Roman fort of Navio, meaning 'on the river', which dates back to the first century AD.

THE PUB

The Woodroffe Arms no website
☎ 01433 623378 **S33 6SB**
Note the pub only serves food after 5pm but, **The Courtyard Café** across the road is a good bet if you fancy a bite to eat.

THE WALK

Walk down Pindale Road beside the pub. Cross the bridge (with a pinfold beyond) and 100 yards later ascend Eccles Lane. To the left is Win Hill.

Guide to Peak District Pub Walks

HOW TO GET THERE: The Woodroffe Arms is on the A6187. In the middle of Hope. It is on the left if you are heading west. **Postcode** S33 6SB

MAP: OS Explorer OL1 The Peak District – Dark Peak area (GR 172835).

PARKING: You can use the pub car park or there is a public car park next to it if you prefer.

After 175 yards climb a stile on the left. Follow the track across the field ahead. In the second field, keep forward alongside woodland on the right. The view opens out. Stay beside the trees, crossing a number of stiles. Continue alongside the trees to cross a footbridge.

2 Keep forward alongside the fence beyond. Continue in this direction across the open field. This contains the remains of the Roman fort Navio. In the last field before the road bear slightly right to the road.

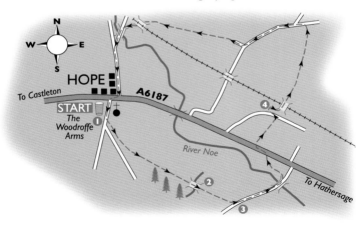

Turn left for 300 yards crossing Bradwell Brook and the River Noe. Beyond the road bridge take the stile on the left. Once in the field, head towards the clump of larger trees projecting into the field. Continue in this direction to a stile 30 yards from the stone outbuilding at the far end of the field. Turn left on the road passing a cottage on the right. Beyond the wood behind the cottage turn right. Walk up the right side of the field. Stay beside the small brook along a fenced path to reach a track.

Turn left. At the end of the terraced cottages turn right. Cross the bridge over the railway line. Bear right beyond, then left to walk up the right side of the field ahead towards Win Hill. Keep in the same direction through a number of fields, ignoring a cross path at one point. Turn left down a tarmac lane. Ignore two driveways to the right. Pass Crabtree Meadow on your left. Turn right on the drive of Farfield Farm and 100 yards later keep left of a pair of dressed stone gateposts, continuing down a track. Stay on the track beside a hedge (ignoring a gate on your left). Enter the trees beyond. Pass under a railway bridge, then pass the cemetery on your right. Subsequently bear left at the lane. Stay on this to cross a bridge to the road. Turn left back to Hope.

PLACES OF INTEREST NEARBY

Travel south-east for around 5 miles and you come to the village of **Hathersage**. Hathersage church has a list of vicars that goes back to 1281, however most of the present building dates back to the 15th century. Legend has it that it is also the resting place of Little John, Robin Hood's trusted friend, who lies under a yew tree to the south of the church. **Castleton** is only a mile away – see page 22 for more information.

Edale Valley from Back Tor

6 Castleton
5.5 miles (8.9 km)

WALK HIGHLIGHTS
There are some steep climbs but you'll be rewarded with some incredible views - including the limestone pinnacles of Winnats Pass and Mam Tor. The latter means 'mother hill', so named because of the landslips on its eastern face which have created some smaller hills beneath it. This is also where it gets the nickname of the 'shivering mountain'.

THE PUB
The Castle Hotel
www.vintageinn.co.uk/restaurants/midlands/thecastlecastleton
☎ 01433 620578 **S33 8WG**

THE WALK
1 From the car park turn right past the Castleton Centre. Head along the road for Winnats Pass. Stay on the road for Treak Cliff Cavern.

2 Rise up the road past the car park for Speedwell Cavern on your left.

20

HOW TO GET THERE: As you drive through Castleton from the east on the A6187 the car park is on the right. **Postcode** S33 8WH

MAP: OS Explorer OL1 Peak District – Dark Peak area (GR 149829).

PARKING: The main public pay & display car park next to the Castleton Centre. Worth getting there early because it gets very busy.

Winnats Pass is half left of you as you go. This dead end road rises and bears right with good views of the Hope Valley. Pass the entrance to Treak Cliff Cavern. At the bus turning area you get a good view of Mam Tor. Keep forward along the old tarmac road, as it winds up the hill.

Continue as far as the sharp left-hand bend. Here turn right onto a track but almost immediately fork left on a path, keeping to the left of the trees. After the first section of trees ignore a fork to the left. This area is Mam Farm. The path takes you on a steady climb to Hollins Cross – you should be heading generally upwards with the top of the hill above on your left. The Hope Valley and the cement works are to your right. After a while another path joins yours from the right. Keep heading upwards.

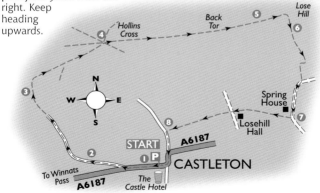

21

Guide to Peak District Pub Walks

4 At Hollins Cross with its viewpoint, turn right along the ridge. The path levels out with more good views, including Edale to your left and Kinder Scout beyond. Stay on the ridge until, with the rocky outcrop of Back Tor directly ahead, you cross over onto the left side of the field boundary to climb up to Back Tor. Proceed along the main path along the ridge.

5 Enter the National Trust property Lose Hill Pike, (also known as Ward's Piece). The flagstone path leads you to the high point of the walk. From the viewpoint bear right downhill on the flagged path.

6 Leave Ward's Piece by climbing a step stile. Keep forward to another stile 50 yards away. Once beyond this, turn left beside the fence on your left. After 200 yards the path bears right slightly, away from the fence, though you keep to the left of the trees. Follow the clear path beside some banking on your left. Fifty yards before a house turn sharp right (for Hope and Castleton). Pass through a wicket gate, heading down the right side of the field beyond. Ignore a cross path as you go. On reaching a track turn right and follow it downhill. Proceed past Castleton Service Reservoir. The gravel track leads down to Spring House. Keep directly forward through this property to join a track immediately beyond.

7 Turn right for Castleton, following the track, with Spring House immediately on your right. Join another track, which rises up to a farm, but turn left here. This track subsequently runs alongside Losehill Hall. At a junction of tracks just beyond the Hall take the footpath directly ahead. Keep on the right side of the field. Cross the small bridge and keep straight ahead, with Winnats Pass in the distance. Keep forward along a track when you reach it.

8 On reaching a T-junction, turn left along a lane leading into Castleton. Keep straight forward, ignoring all lanes to the left and right. At the main street, turn right, back to the car park.

PLACES OF INTEREST NEARBY

Visit the four caves which make up the **Show Caverns** in Castleton. www.visitcastleton.co.uk Then there are the remains of 11th-century **Peveril Castle**. www.english-heritage.org.uk

Kinder Scout

7 Longshaw
3 miles (4.8 km)

WALK HIGHLIGHTS
Distant views towards Win Hill, Lose Hill and the moorland plateau of Kinder Scout. There are also impressive views of Carl Wark, an ancient hillfort, and Higger, a gritstone tor, as you look right when you reach the driveway of Longshaw Lodge which was a hunting lodge and is now owned by the National Trust.

THE PUB
The Grouse Inn www.thegrouseinn-derbyshire.co.uk
☎ 01433 630423 **S11 7TZ**

THE WALK
From the Grouse Inn turn left up the A625 for 40 yards. Pass through the bridlegate on the right. Cross the field (keeping the marshy area to your right) towards another bridlegate. Follow the bridleway to enter the Eastern Moors Estate. Pass through some silver birches. Where the path splits at the base of some boulders turn left. Follow the grassy

Guide to Peak District Pub Walks

HOW TO GET THERE: From the traffic lights at Calver Crossroads take the A625 heading north. After 350 yards fork right to stay on the A625. Stay on this for 2½ miles, climbing steadily to reach the Grouse Inn on the left. **Postcode** S11 7TZ

MAP: OS Explorer OL24 The Peak District – White Peak area.

PARKING: There is a small lay-by just down the road from The Grouse Inn and two National Trust car parks nearby.

bridleway slightly uphill. The view on the left opens out with Eyam Moor surmounted by a transmitter. To the right of this are Lose Hill and Win Hill with Kinder Scout beyond. Pass through a bridlegate onto White Edge Moor, part of the Longshaw Estate.

2 Stay on the bridleway as it rises and bears right round a hillock. It then straightens out. Continue past White Edge Lodge to your left. As you proceed look out for the distinctive flat top of Higger Tor to your left with Carl Wark (an ancient hillfort) in front of it. Before long the bridleway joins the gravel driveway to the lodge. Walk on this in the same direction as before.

3 At the road, cross the grass triangle carefully. Keep forward to the gate gaining access to the area known as Wooden Pole. The pole would have been a marker for travellers in days gone by. Follow the wide grassy path descending gently to the left of the pole. Ignore another path coming in sharply from the left. Continue to a gate with beech trees beyond. Enter this wood to walk behind the buildings of Longshaw Lodge. Ignore all other paths until you bend round to the left to reach the access road to the lodge.

4 Cross the driveway, descend some steps and turn left in front of the lodge. After passing through a small gate you stand under five yew trees. Avoid the path descending gently to the right, proceed forward through another small gate and keep on the track ahead.

5 Stay on this track. Keep forward where another crosses it. The track

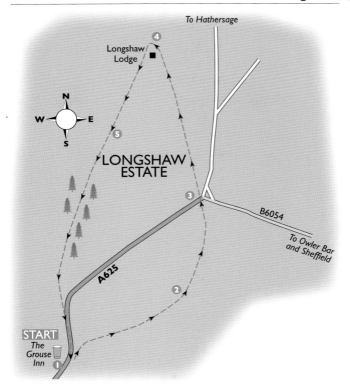

brings you back to the A625. Turn right back to the pub.

PLACES OF INTEREST NEARBY

The **Old House Museum**, in Bakewell, is a typical 16th-century yeoman's house, now home to a small museum with an exhibition of local life and artefacts and is worth a visit. www.oldhousemuseum.org.uk

Hall Hill Water Troughs

8 Eyam
2.3 miles (3.6 km)

WALK HIGHLIGHTS

Eyam (pronounced 'eem') is best known for the resilience of its residents in cutting themselves off from the outside world to try and stop the bubonic plague from spreading in the 17th century. The walk takes note of this, passing or visiting a number of relevant sites. There's a relatively steep climb near point 2 to reach Mompesson's Well, where neighbouring villagers left food and medicine for the residents of Eyam to collect. The well is named after the local minister at the time, William Mompesson.

THE PUB

The Miners Arms www.theminersarmseyam.co.uk
☎ 01433 630853 **S32 5RG**

❶ THE WALK

With your back to the pub entrance turn left along Water Lane, then left again at the main road onto The Causeway. Proceed along the road

HOW TO GET THERE: From the A623 take the B6521 heading north into Eyam. In the centre of the village bear left into Water Lane. The pub is visible ahead. **Postcode** S32 5RG

MAP: OS Explorer OL24 The Peak District – White Peak area (GR 219765).

PARKING: In the pub car park, this is just beyond the pub and behind it.

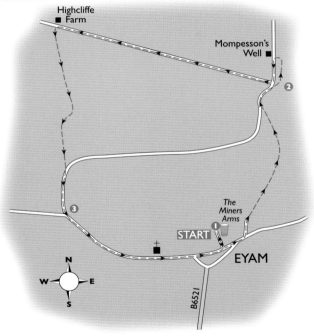

passing Miners Arms Croft and the Wesleyan Reform church. After this turn left into Riley Back Lane and follow it round to the right after 10 yards. This tarmac access road leads uphill before downgrading to a path leading along the edge of a wood. Where the path splits take the right fork uphill and ascend the wide stony path. This is a lovely path under broad-leaved trees though it changes character under some conifers. At the top of the plantation keep on the path. This starts to lead uphill until you're walking along the top of the wood. Bear right up to the road.

2 Turn right for 75 yards to the Bretton road. Before you take the Bretton road though, walk uphill for 100 yards to visit Mompesson's Well. Return to the Bretton road. Follow this for ½ a mile passing the chimney of Ladywash Mine on the right. Continue to Highcliffe Farm and Highcliffe Barns. Turn sharp left here and descend the track until it becomes a tarmac access road. Stay on this to reach the corner of a road. Continue downhill to pass Eyam Museum on the right. Beyond that pass Hall Hill Troughs – an early example of a public water supply.

3 At the bottom of the hill – 30 yards beyond the troughs – turn left into the main street. Pass Eyam Hall on the left and some stocks on the right. Then pass the Sheep Roast and immediately afterwards Rose Cottage where members of the Thorpe family died during the plague. Then pass Plague Cottage where the first victim died. Once past the church the road will bring you back into the centre of the village. Turn left at Water Lane back to the pub.

PLACES OF INTEREST NEARBY

Eyam Museum tells of the villagers' self-sacrifice in their attempt to prevent the plague from spreading. www.eyam-museum.org.uk Alternatively, there is **Eyam Hall and Craft Centre**, an interesting Jacobean house with local crafts and café. www.nationaltrust.org.uk

9 Miller's Dale

4.8 miles (7.6 km)

WALK HIGHLIGHTS

The route takes in the lovely village of Wormhill, with its memorial to James Brindley (1716-1772), who was one of the foremost engineers of English canals. You'll also see the impressive scale of Old Moor and Tunstead quarries and then descend into Miller's Dale itself and stroll beside the River Wye.

THE PUB

The Anglers Rest www.anglersrestmillersdale.co.uk
☎ 01298 871323 **SK17 8SN**

THE WALK

Walk to the car park entrance and turn sharp left on the path, climbing the steps. Follow the walled path ahead for 300 yards. Then bear half right up to the road. Turn left along the lane for ⅓ mile.

Immediately beyond a farm gate on your right pass through the squeezer

Guide to Peak District Pub Walks

HOW TO GET THERE: From the A6 westwards from the Taddington bypass. Pass the Waterloo pub on your left. After ½ a mile turn right on the B6049 and continue down into the valley. **Postcode** SK17 8SN

MAP: OS Explorer OL24 The Peak District – White Peak area (GR 139733).

PARKING: After crossing the River Wye, turn left uphill to Miller's Dale car park.

stile. Walk along the right side of the small field, bearing half left in the second field. Keep in the same direction across the corner of the third field. Keep in the same direction across the fourth field to reach a walled track. Turn left for 5 yards, then right through another squeezer. Stay in the same direction in the fifth field to reach a step-over in the far corner. With your back to the stile in the sixth field, walk to the far left corner. Here there's a gate. Follow the track beyond as it bends round to the left to reach the entrance to St Margaret's church. Continue to the road.

❸ At the road in Wormhill, turn right along a path below the road. Pass the old stocks and head up the main street for 300 yards. Turn left up the driveway to Old Hall Farm, following the Pennine Bridleway. At the top of the farmyard bear half left through a gate. Follow the stony track leading uphill. Keep forward, walking beside a wall on your right, as the track levels out before going downhill. Follow it until you reach two farm gates side by side. Pass through the right-hand one, walking beside the wall on your left beyond. Continue along the walled track at the end of the field to reach a lane.

❹ Turn left here (there's a water trough directly ahead). After 300 yards bear left along the tarmac bridleway, with trees on your right. Continue for 400 yards and, as the bridleway bears right, uphill, keep straight forward along the grassy verge to reach and enter the end of the narrow field on your left. Walk to the bottom corner and turn right through a small gate. With your back to the gate, aim slightly left towards a gap in the wall (just to the left of the valley bottom). Pass through this and, keeping in the same direction, pass through a squeezer between a

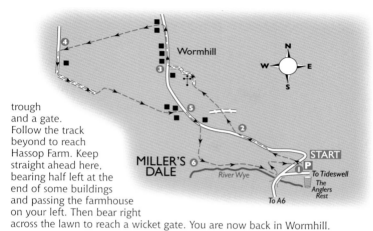

trough
and a gate.
Follow the track
beyond to reach
Hassop Farm. Keep
straight ahead here,
bearing half left at the
end of some buildings
and passing the farmhouse
on your left. Then bear right
across the lawn to reach a wicket gate. You are now back in Wormhill.

Turn right down the road for 75 yards to turn right again down the footpath for Cheedale and Blackwell. This brings you to the Derbyshire Wildlife Trust Reserve. Descend until you come out from under the trees. Ignore a path turning sharp right here. Continue forward along the level path into the open. Then descend a (sometimes slippery) path to the River Wye.

Turn left along the riverside path. The river should be on your right for a good ½ mile. Ignore some steps on your left leading back to Miller's Dale Station. Pass under the bridge and proceed until you reach a road. Immediately before the road turn left up the steps back towards the car park. Bear right to reach the station building and the car park.

PLACES OF INTEREST NEARBY

It is worth looking round **Tideswell church** which is known as the 'Cathedral of the Peak'. It is one of the largest in the area and was completed in the 14th century. It contains some interesting carvings and memorials.

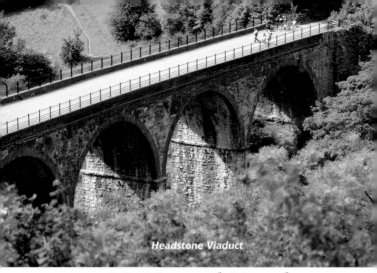

Headstone Viaduct

10 Monsal Head

2.3 miles (3.6 km)

WALK HIGHLIGHTS

Monsal Head must be one of the most photographed views in the Peak District, and this walk thoroughly explores it. It's a figure of eight walk, but the crossing point is some 30 yards above the valley floor, so you don't actually step on the path you've used previously. On the return leg you use the Monsal Trail which originally carried the railway line from Matlock to Buxton. You will also see the impressive Headstone Viaduct, which was built by the Midland Railway in 1863, and is 300 ft long with five 50 ft span arches. Although when it was built it was thought to destroy the landscape it is now considered a beautiful part of the dale.

THE PUB

The Stable Bar www.monsalhead.com
☎ 01629 640250 **DE45 1NL**

HOW TO GET THERE: Monsal Head is a couple of miles north-west of Ashford in the Water on the B6465. **Postcode** DE45 1NL

MAP: OS Explorer OL24 The Peak District – White Peak area (GR 185715).

PARKING: Behind the Monsal Head Hotel in the district council pay & display car park.

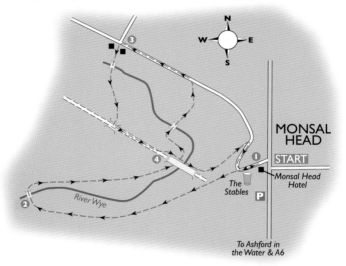

THE WALK

Standing with your back to the front of the Monsal Head Hotel, walk left to the Monsal View Café. In front of this is a marvellous view with the viaduct below. Take the path for Ashford and Monsal Dale. After 10 or 12 yards the path forks; take the lower one. The path levels out before descending to the River Wye. Keep beside this until you reach and cross a footbridge.

Guide to Peak District Pub Walks

2 Turn right upstream beyond the bridge. You pass a weir on your right before eventually coming out, with the viaduct ahead of you. Pass through a stile by a gate beneath the viaduct. Follow the path underneath it. This wheels left, with the river on your right, to bring you to a footbridge. Cross the river for the second time. You reach Netherdale Farm. Keep left of the buildings and then swing left on the drive to the road. Turn left along the road for 500 yards.

3 On reaching the crossroads, turn left, back to the river (look out for the trout as you cross it!). Bear left up the old lane and stay on it under the Monsal Trail. Fork left onto the Trail but turn right along it so that you're walking with the river down below to your left. You pass the remains of Monsal Dale Station. Eventually you reach the viaduct and cross it.

4 Keep forward towards the tunnel. Just before it, turn left up a path and keep going to reach a T-junction of paths. Turn right up here back to the Monsal Head Hotel.

PLACES OF INTEREST NEARBY
Thornbridge Hall in Ashford in the Water is a couple of miles away and best known for its stunning 12 acres of formal gardens. They were designed in the 1890s to produce a vision of *'1,000 shades of green'* as seen from the hall's bedroom windows. There is also a further 90 acres of woodland and parkland to explore, a café and plant nursery. Check opening times. www.thornbridgehall.co.uk

The Emperor Fountain at Chatsworth House

11 Chatsworth Estate

7 miles (11.3 km)

WALK HIGHLIGHTS

Although you won't get this close to the house on the walk, you will see the Emperor Lake, which, by gravity alone, feeds the impressive Emperor Fountain in the grounds of the House. Designed by Joseph Paxton in 1843, this is said to be the tallest gravity-fed fountain in the world, capable of reaching 295 ft in height.

THE PUB

The Robin Hood Inn www.robinhoodinnbaslow.co.uk
☎ 01246 583186 **DE45 1PQ**

THE WALK

From the car park walk back to the A619 and turn right. Sixty yards later cross the road to a concessionary path on your left. Go over a stream. When the path levels, cross a track (which you will rejoin later) heading for Beeley via Swiss Lake. Cross a ladder stile, taking the path alongside a plantation on your left. You then rise up above the busy A619. Keep forward along this path before crossing into the rocky corner of a field

Guide to Peak District Pub Walks

HOW TO GET THERE: The pub is at the junction of the B6050 and A619 as it heads westward from Chesterfield to Baslow. **Postcode** DE45 1PQ

MAP: OS Explorer OL24 The Peak District – White Peak area (GR 281721).

PARKING: Park in the Birchen Edge pay and display car park beside the Robin Hood Inn. Get there early as there is limited space.

and immediately take the small squeezer stile on your right. Walk a few yards to the path and turn left. Eventually the path leads into a field; keep forward along the right side of it. This brings you to a high step stile over a wall. Cross this and keep forward with a high wall on your left.

2 Climb another tall step stile into plantation land. Follow the path to bear right along the track. Keep forward where tracks cross. You should now be following a tarmac driveway. Ignore a concessionary path sharp right (for Baslow). At a crossroads of tracks turn left. Shortly afterwards keep forward when tracks join from both sides. Ignore a track forking right. On reaching Emperor Lake fork left, crossing the small concrete bridge to continue on the gravel track and subsequently reach Swiss Lake on your left. Swiss Cottage is on the far side.

3 Continue as before, ignoring the private access to Swiss Cottage on your left. The track gently swings right, with a farm a field away to your left. The track then swings left. Keep forward at the crossroads of tracks. A high step stile leads you out of Chatsworth Park and onto Rabbit Warren Edge. Follow the track in front as it rises. Away to your left is a plantation. When the end of it is parallel to you (to your left, and just before the top of the climb) turn left along a concessionary footpath. This will take you towards the right side of the plantation, though you soon swing slightly left. You reach a small gate near the plantation. On the far side of this, walk up the right side of a wall, with the plantation beyond the wall.

4 Where the wall bends left, follow the track, keeping the wall on your left. Hob Hurst's House (an ancient burial site named after a mythical elf who haunted the nearby woods) is to your far right. On reaching a stone outbuilding beyond a stone wall, swing right on the track. When the wall bends left, keep forward on the track, heading towards the A619.

Cross a small stone bridge before, a few yards later, turning left along a path for Robin Hood. Slowly descend to walk beside a brook with the road to your right. Follow the path by the brook before turning sharp left up some steps. Bear right at the top of the steps to walk above the brook through the bracken. Then head away slightly from the brook. Cross a step stile, following the waymarked path to reach the track mentioned at the beginning. Turn sharp right to return the way you came.

PLACES OF INTEREST NEARBY

Chatsworth House is renowned for its amazing art collection spanning 4,000 years, from ancient Roman and Egyptian sculpture, and masterpieces by Rembrandt and Reynolds, to work of more modern artists including Lucian Freud. The farm and gardens are also worth exploring. www.chatsworth.org

Strip fields near Chelmorton

12 Chelmorton

2.8 miles (4.4 km)

WALK HIGHLIGHTS

Chelmorton is famous for its ancient field system and is the highest village in the Peak District with the church standing 1,200 ft above sea level. The church chancel, tower and spire are mid 18th-century additions to the original limestone church built by the Normans 500 years earlier. Bronze Age tumuli on the summit of Chelmorton Low suggest early human habitation in the area. The walk itself is a fairly flat route with fine views to be enjoyed.

THE PUB

The Church Inn www.thechurchinn.co.uk
☎ 01298 85319 **SK17 9SL**

THE WALK

1 From the Church Inn walk down the road for 50 yards. Opposite the road heading left, turn right along a gravel track. Stay on this, bearing left where the right fork proceeds into the farmyard. The old field system

HOW TO GET THERE: 1¼ miles past the Taddington Bypass on the A6 turn left on the A5270. Look out for the signs for Chelmorton on the left. The pub is at the highest point of the village by the church. **Postcode** SK17 9SL

MAP: OS Explorer OL24 The Peak District – White Peak area (GR 115703).

PARKING: Carefully and considerately near the pub or lower down on the village street. There is no public car park.

can be seen to your left. Keep on the gravel track. It forms part of the Midshires Way – a long-distance footpath running for over 220 miles from the Ridgeway northwards.

When you reach the road there are two tracks opposite. Take the one on the left (Caxterway Lane). Ahead are the higher parts of Buxton but

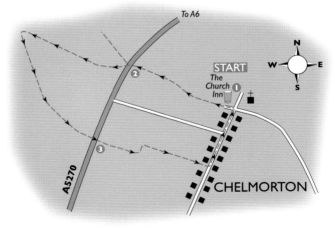

you'll also see some of the quarries. Ignore the first 'green lane' to the left but take the second one – just after a bend in the track. Away to the right you'll get a glimpse of Back Dale. Proceed along the green lane but ignore another that forks right beyond a farm gate. Eventually you arrive back at the road.

3 Cross this to the green lane opposite. This is rather more tree-lined than the others. Ignore the first green lane to the left. Shortly afterwards follow the lane round to the left. After 100 yards turn right over a stile into a field and walk down the right side. To your left is Chelmorton Low – a 'low' being a high piece of ground! In the next field, walk down the left side. Beyond this, walk down the path beside the house, through the garden. Then walk down the drive to the road. Turn left at the road back to the pub.

PLACES OF INTEREST NEARBY

Buxton Museum and Art Gallery is well worth a visit and only a few miles away. The 'Wonders of the Peak' exhibition gives a history of the area and there are fossils and archaeological finds from all over the Peak District. There is also a collection of 19th and 20th-century art.
www.derbyshire.gov.uk/leisure/buxton_museum

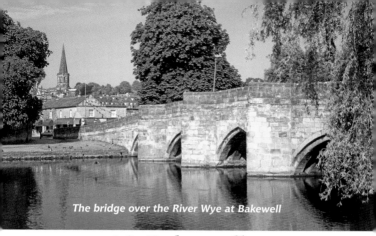

The bridge over the River Wye at Bakewell

13 Bakewell

4 miles (6.4 km)

WALK HIGHLIGHTS

Bakewell is probably best known throughout the world because of a tart which is in fact a pudding! The origin of the tart is shrouded in confusion. On the walk you'll see gorgeous scenery with a view towards the limestone ridge of Longstone Edge. The route follows the Monsal Trail, along an old railway line and crosses the River Wye.

THE PUB

The Peacock www.peacockbakewell.com
☎ 01629 813635 **DE45 1DS**

THE WALK

From the Bakewell Bridge car park, head across the main bridge and cross the road to the Castle Inn. Proceed along Castle Street to the right of the pub. At the end bear left alongside the stream. Where this comes out onto the road, keep forward to the A6. Turn right passing Victoria Mill. After 200 yards, turn right to cross Holme Bridge (an old packhorse

Guide to Peak District Pub Walks

HOW TO GET THERE: Head south on the A619 and turn left just before the bridge into Bakewell. Take the first right-hand fork and the car park will be on your right. **Postcode** DE45 1AQ

HOW TO GET TO THE PUB: Cross the Wye on the A619 heading south into Bakewell. Take the first left and the pub is immediately on your left. **Postcode** DE45 1DS

MAP: OS Explorer OL24 The Peak District – White Peak area (GR 219686).

PARKING: Bakewell Bridge Car Park or one of the other public car parks in the vicinity.

bridge). Keep forward (ignoring the road to the left and right). After 60 yards the path rises through the remains of various buildings. Stay on this partly concreted track to reach a farm gate with fields beyond.

2 Pass through the gate. Follow the bridleway along the gravel track. Where it swings left towards the old quarry keep forward to the top corner of the field. Keep to the right of the dewpond to reach a walled track. Proceed up this. Longstone Edge appears ahead. After cresting the hill, walk through a large field with the wall on your right-hand side and a fence on the left. Keep on the bridleway to reach the Monsal Trail.

3 With Toll Bar Cottage 100 yards in front of you, turn right along the Trail for 1¼ miles. This was the railway line that ran from Matlock, through the Peak District, up to Buxton. This provides a leisurely walk to Bakewell Station which was closed in 1967.

4 Stay on the Trail beyond Bakewell Station to pass under a bridge almost immediately. In ¼ mile you reach another bridge. Don't pass under this – climb up the steps on the left. Turn right to cross the bridge. Follow the path down the left side of the field beyond to a driveway at the bottom of the field which takes you to a road. Turn right at the road. Immediately beyond Long Meadow House turn left into the car park

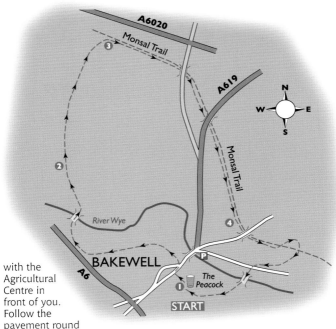

with the Agricultural Centre in front of you. Follow the pavement round the right side of the car park to a footbridge. Cross this, then a second one over the River Wye. Keep forward for 30 yards from the bridge you've just crossed. Turn right to the Peacock.

PLACES OF INTEREST NEARBY

The impressive medieval **Haddon Hall** is a little further along the A6 south-east of Bakewell. Parts of the house date from the 12th century. There are Elizabethan terraced gardens and it overlooks the River Wye. www.haddonhall.co.uk

The River Lathkill

14 Over Haddon

4.8 miles (7.6 km)

WALK HIGHLIGHTS

With the Lathkil Hotel sitting proudly above Lathkill Dale (yes, they're spelled differently) you have another marvellous Peak District pub. Over Haddon is where the Wildgooses lived in the 19th century and earlier – so that's one claim to fame for the area! Seriously though, Over Haddon is a beautiful limestone village, and this walk lets you see some of the area both above, and below ground.

THE PUB

The Lathkil Hotel www.lathkil.co.uk
☎ 01629 812501 **DE45 1JE**

THE WALK

Please note: you will not be able to walk this route on a Wednesday between October and January as a concessionary path in Lathkill Dale is closed.

HOW TO GET THERE: Take the B5055 south-west from Bakewell, before turning left a mile outside Bakewell for Over Haddon. Follow signs in the village for the car park. **Postcode** DE45 1JE

MAP: OS Explorer OL24 The Peak District – White Peak area (GR 204664).

PARKING: Use the district council pay & display car park at the western end of the village.

Turn left out of the public car park entrance, then left again at the T-junction (along Monyash Road). Stay on this lane for nearly a mile. Where the road forks, go left along the minor lane. Nearly another mile later, at the right-hand 90° bend, turn left along the drive for Haddon Grove Farm.

The footpath goes right through the farmyard. Keep straight forward on reaching the far end of the farmhouse and leave the farmyard at the far end down the right side of a breeze-block building. Keep forward to pass through a squeezer stile in the line of trees. Leave the trees 4 or 5 yards later by another stile. Head forward through the field ahead, 15 yards from a wall on your right. Beyond the valley ahead is One Ash

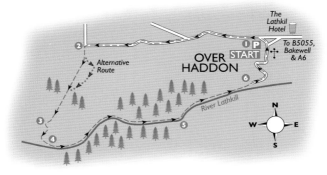

Grange – for 200 years between the 1690s and the 1890s this was the home of the Bowman family, who were Quakers. Pass through a stile and gently descend.

③ Pass through a wooden kissing gate to enter Natural England's Derbyshire Dales Nature Reserve. There are fine views from here – it's a place where a stop is justly deserved. Turn half left from the kissing gate and look for a path a few yards ahead of you on the right. Zigzag down this steep path into Lathkill Dale itself.

④ Turn left along the path in the valley bottom and head downstream. The River Lathkill is one of the cleanest and clearest of rivers – assuming it is running. During the summer it dries up, with any water disappearing underground. Pass through a gate into Palmerston Wood – this concessionary path is closed on a Wednesday between October and January. It is nice and shady in hot weather. Eventually, look out for a bridge on your right. Cross this to Bateman's House. Do take the opportunity to climb down the metal ladder and wind the dynamo. Then look at the water below. You will feel cold down here even though you're only a few feet below ground. Once finished return, over the bridge, back to the path.

⑤ Pass through a couple of gateposts to come out in the open but, just before you do, 10 yards before the gateposts look out on your right for the sough (pronounced 'suff'), from which water runs out of the old lead mine nearby.

⑥ Eventually you reach Lathkill Lodge. Head up the lane to the left of it. Zigzag all the way back up to the car park.

PLACES OF INTEREST NEARBY

Just over five miles away is **Caudwell's Mill**, at Rowsley, where there's a Grade II listed working mill and craft shops. www.caudwellsmill.co.uk

The Hanging Stone

15 Wincle

4.5 miles (7.3 km)

WALK HIGHLIGHTS

The route is a bit rockier than some walks, but you'll be rewarded with fine views and fascinating sights. At Point 3 you'll have the option to go off the path to visit Lud's Church, a damp, fern-filled chasm, some 30 ft deep. It is named after Walter de Ludauk, a leader of a 14th-century religious group. You'll also see the precarious rock outcrop, Hanging Stone.

THE PUB

The Ship Inn www.theshipinnwincle.co.uk

☎ 01260 227217 **SK11 0QE**

THE WALK

Walk down the road away from the Ship to cross the River Dane by the road bridge. Take the path on the left for Gradbach Via Dane Valley.

Guide to Peak District Pub Walks

HOW TO GET THERE: Wincle is just off the A54 between Buxton and Congleton. Approaching from the north-east, turn off left at the crossroads, signed for Wincle. At the church turn left, signposted to Danebridge. **Postcode** SK11 0QE

MAP: OS Explorer OL24 The Peak District – White Peak area (GR 962653).

PARKING: On the roadside just below the Ship Inn.

After 50 yards climb over the stile and head up the stone steps towards 'Hanging Stone' on your right, and 200 yards later ignore a footpath turning sharp right. The path you're on crosses a plank footbridge over a stream. Keep forward to climb the stile into the field. Ahead of you is Hanging Stone. Walk across the field, keeping to the left of the farm ahead. As you go, keep to the left of a stone in the middle of the field, aiming for the stile beyond. Turn half right uphill beyond the stile. On reaching a track above the farm turn right over a stile passing below Hanging Stone itself. Ahead is a view of The Roaches, including the rocky outcrop of Hen Cloud. On reaching a cattle grid ignore the concessionary path on your left leading uphill to Hanging Stone (unless you want to visit it and return to this point).

2 Keep forward into the open area beyond and bear slightly left to follow the footpath beyond a farm gate. Walk along beside the trees on your right, passing a house. Continue walking between a fence on your left and a wall on your right. Pass through another farm gate and bear left up the wide grassy path for Gradbach. This soon bears left and becomes a sunken path.

3 On reaching another gate, cross the stile and keep forward, still for Gradbach, ignoring the path to the right for Roaches. Stay on this bridleway for ½ mile until it forks by a rocky outcrop on your left. The walk will continue along the left fork – but feel free to follow the right fork for Lud's Church about 250 yards away, and return to this spot.

4 Your route takes you down to the River Dane, where you should turn

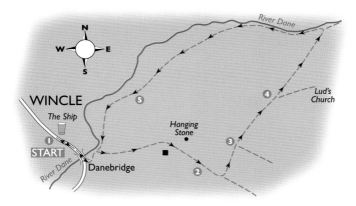

sharp left. Follow the path with the river on your right. Where the path splits, take the right fork beside the river. Stay on the path for a good ½ mile until you leave the woodland by a stile. The path you're on rises so that you enter a field. Keep forward to climb a stile and keep on the path between fences. Cross a driveway and continue between fences on the path beyond. Continue on the obvious path, which stays at basically the same height. On reaching a tarmac driveway bear right downhill. Pass the property below on your right. Just beyond, walk along a level path, dropping slightly, beside a tumbledown wall on your left. Enter the woodland again.

Subsequently ignore a grassy track heading up and forking left; keep on towards the river heading down. Leave the wood by a wicket gate, following the obvious path with the river to your right. On reaching the road bridge go uphill to your right to return to the Ship Inn.

PLACES OF INTEREST NEARBY

Some 4 miles south of Danebridge, is **Tittesworth Water**, where there is an outdoor play area, birdwatching near the reservoir, and for the more adventurous the chance to hire canoes and kayaks.
www.visittittesworth.co.uk

The Dove Valley Path

16 Crowdecote

2.5 miles (4 km)

WALK HIGHLIGHTS

The walk starts in Crowdecote (pronounced 'Croudicot') which is just inside Derbyshire. It's a good stroll taking in the River Dove and some interesting views. After walking up the Derbyshire side of the river you'll soon cross into Staffordshire at Beggar's Bridge. As you get to this point you'll have noticed the distinctive shapes of Chrome Hill and Parkhouse Hill further up the valley. There is one section at point 3 which is downhill and can be very muddy – so avoid this walk in wet weather or after rain.

THE PUB

The Pack Horse Inn www.thepack-horseinn.co.uk
☎ 01298 83618 **SK17 0DB**
The pub is closed on Mondays and Tuesdays.

THE WALK

1 With your back to the inn turn right on the road then almost immediately left on another. After 100 yards, take the track on the left for Glutton Bridge. Follow this as it bears right, walking through the farmyard of

HOW TO GET THERE: From the A515 at the crossroads west of Monyash, take the road heading west for Longnor. Stay on this road until it zigzags steeply downhill. The Pack Horse Inn is on the left in the hamlet of Crowdecote. **Postcode** SK17 0DB

MAP: OS Explorer OL24 The Peak District – White Peak area (GR 101652).

PARKING: It is all right to use the pub car park, but please let the landlord know first.

Meadow Farm. Keep the buildings on your left. Stay on the track beyond the farm. Where it enters an open field, walk towards the far right corner and along the right side of the field beyond.

This brings you to a stile (with a tarmac driveway a few yards ahead). Turn left here down the narrow field. Cross the wooden Beggar's Bridge over the infant River Dove. Keep in the same direction beyond and rise up the field ahead. Keep forward towards a building, part way up the bankside ahead. Bear left behind the building and rise up the track. This climbs quite steeply to Longnor. Turn left at the road as you reach the houses. Then at the main road which enters the village, turn left again. (If you want to explore Longnor then turn right here.)

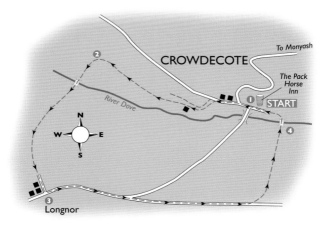

3 Continue for 300 yards along the main road after turning left. Then fork right along the Sheen road. Continue along here for ½ a mile enjoying the views to your left as you proceed. Opposite Edgetop, on the right, take the footpath on your left. This heads diagonally right downhill. This can be very muddy. Pass through the hawthorns to reach a wall, going through a wicket gate. Turn left and then almost immediately right. Walk down the left side of the field beyond. Keep forward in the same direction when the field opens out on your left.

4 Cross another bridge back over the Dove. Walk forward for 20 yards then turn left along the track which brings you back to Crowdecote and the Pack Horse Inn.

PLACES OF INTEREST NEARBY

About a mile away is **Longnor Craft Centre and Coffee Shop** selling homemade cakes and light lunches. There are over 70 craft contributors including card makers, artists, photographers, potters and jewellery makers. www.longnorcrafts.co.uk

Biggin Hall

17 Biggin by Hartington

3 miles (4.8 km)

WALK HIGHLIGHTS

Biggin is a small village set high in the spectacular White Peak landscape surrounded by farmsteads and agricultural land. About half of this route follows the Tissington Trail which gives you an ideal opportunity to view the hills of Dovedale away to your left. On the return leg of the walk you pass 17th-century Biggin Hall, now a popular country house hotel. Incidentally, it's Biggin by Hartington because less than ten miles away there's another Biggin – Biggin by Hulland.

THE PUB

The Waterloo Inn www.waterlooinnbiggin.com
☎ 01298 84284 **SK17 0DH**

THE WALK

From the Waterloo Inn turn left up the road. Ignore the road to the right at the church. Turn left on the path 60 yards later (having ignored Percival Close). The path leads into fields behind the village. Walk up

Guide to Peak District Pub Walks

HOW TO GET THERE: From the junction of the A515 with the A5012 at Newhaven head south on the A515. Half a mile later, turn right for Biggin. The pub is on the right at the western end of the village. **Postcode** SK17 0DH

MAP: OS Explorer OL24 The Peak District – White Peak area (GR 153595).

PARKING: You can park in the pub car park with permission, or park on the road near the church.

the left side of the first one. Head diagonally across the second field to the top left corner. Keep on the right side of the third to pass through a wicket gate and bear right, up to the Tissington Trail.

2 Turn left on the Trail. A mile later you reach Ruby Wood, planted to mark the Peak Park's 40th anniversary. The wood is in an enclosure named after the horse that was used by the local Ranger some years ago. Back on the Trail, press on to pass under the road bridge.

3 After ¼ mile (just before a picnic area/car park) turn very sharp left through a wicket gate off the Trail onto a path between walls. This runs parallel to (but above) the Trail on your left for a short way. Keep on the left side of the fields beyond until you reach a walled track. Follow this to White House Farm and a tarmac drive to the left. Follow this to the crossroads. Walk straight across and proceed along the main street of Heathcote. This eventually becomes a track which you should follow. Ignore a footpath sign next to the barn on the left. Beyond the houses where the track bears left, keep forward through the wicket gate and cross the field to the stile opposite. In the second field head to the far left corner. Proceed on the right side of the third field. Then in the fourth field continue in the direction of the church tower, bearing slightly left away from the wall on your right. Climb over the stile in the corner of the field and keep forward through the car park for the holiday cottages and holiday park, to walk down the gravel driveway with various buildings on your right including 17th-century Biggin Hall. At the road beyond turn left back to the Waterloo Inn.

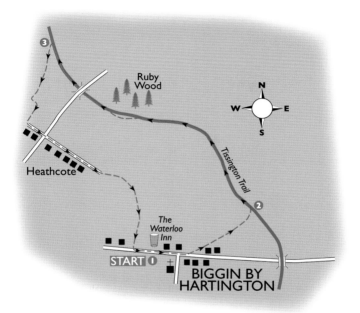

PLACES OF INTEREST NEARBY

Head north-west to the **Old Cheese Shop** in Hartington. One of the few places where true Stilton can be made legally.
www.hartingtoncheeseshop.co.uk
Alternatively, travel a few miles north on the A515 to **Parsley Hay**, where you can hire a bike to ride on the Tissington Trail you've just walked. www.peakdistrict.gov.uk

Minninglow Hill

18 Minninglow

3.8 miles (6 km)

WALK HIGHLIGHTS

This is a fairly steady and evocative stroll in the White Peak area. You'll cross the trackbed of the former Cromford and High Peak Railway line which closed in 1967 and was adapted in the 1970s to form the High Peak Trail. There's also a marvellous view of Minninglow towards the end of the walk. This prominent landmark was the site of a number of burials over 2,000 years ago.

THE PUB

The Sycamore Inn www.robinsonsbrewery.com/sycamoreparwich
☎ 01335 390212 **DE6 1QL**

THE WALK

1 Walk to the lane at the eastern end of the car park as though you were going to cross it to continue along the Trail towards Cromford. Don't follow the Trail, though – turn left along the narrow lane. After about 700 yards, on a gentle left-hand bend, a track joins the road

HOW TO GET THERE: From Pikehall on the A5012 between Newhaven and Grangemill, turn south for Parwich. After just over ½ mile turn left for the Minninglow car park. **Postcode** DE4 2PN

HOW TO GET TO THE PUB: From the car park turn right and then left to head south for two miles or so. Follow the signs into Parwich where you will find the Sycamore Inn, next to the church. **Postcode** DE6 1QL

MAP: OS Explorer OL24 The Peak District – White Peak area (GR 194582).

PARKING: Minninglow car park.

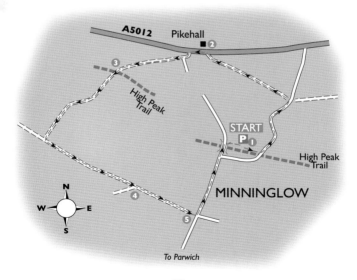

from the right; turn left through a gate to follow a track downhill into Pikehall.

2 On reaching the main road turn left along the verge as far as the road for Parwich. Follow this as it winds right, then left. On the left-hand bend take the gravel lane leading steadily uphill. As you ascend this, ahead (slightly right), you will see Aleck Low, nearly 1,300 ft above sea level.

3 On reaching the High Peak Trail (which is also the Pennine Bridleway), cross this (unless you want a shorter walk back to the car park, in which case you would turn left along the Trail). Continue along the gravel track, which rises steadily uphill. After $2/3$ of a mile Cardlemere Lane joins yours from the right. Turn left and follow the walled track beyond. When the track enters an open field, keep forward on the track, shortly walking beside a wall on your right. The views have opened out by now, with Minninglow, the tree-topped hill, being prominent.

4 On reaching another track joining from sharp right, ignore it and head forward towards Minninglow.

5 After ½ mile you reach a tarmac lane (having passed an isolated cottage on your right). Turn left here back to the car park.

PLACES OF INTEREST NEARBY
Winster Market House, believed to have been erected in the 16th century, is open to visitors between April and October. Information boards on the first floor give the history of the house and village. www.nationaltrust.co.uk/winster-market-house
Slightly further away is **Carsington Water** run by Severn Trent Water. There is a Visitor Centre and an excellent interactive exhibition explaining everything you need to know about water. The reservoir is home to hundreds of birds, including species rarely found elsewhere in the UK. There are also craft shops, an adventure playground, a sailing club and cycle hire centre. www.visitcarsington.co.uk

Viator's Bridge

19 Alstonefield

3.5 miles (5.7 km)

WALK HIGHLIGHTS

The lovely village of Alstonefield and the marvellous scenery of the valley of the river Dove are featured on this short but slightly challenging walk. I'd say it will take a couple of hours, but it could be longer if you go slowly and savour it. At Milldale you come to Viator's Bridge and a small National Trust barn, which provides some information about the area. Look out for dippers in the river. They are the small brown birds with a white bib that are constantly 'dipping' as they stand on stones in the water. Viator's Bridge is for ever connected with Izaak Walton who wrote *The Compleat Angler* in the 17th century. Walton regularly fished these waters.

THE PUB

The George www.thegeorgeatalstonefield.com
☎ 01335 310205 **DE6 2FX**

Guide to Peak District Pub Walks

HOW TO GET THERE: Alstonefield is 3 miles south of Hartington as the crow flies and is reached from the A515 west of Alsop en le Dale or from the B5054 at Hulme End. **Postcode** DE6 2FY

MAP: OS Explorer OL24 The Peak District – White Peak area (GR 131557).

PARKING: In the small public conveniences car park.

THE WALK

1 From the car park turn right up the road. Follow this round to the left. Pass the triangular green (opposite the George) on your right. This road is signed for Lode Mill and Ashbourne. You will soon be leaving Alstonefield. Ignore a walled track/footpath on your left for Narrow Dale and Gipsy Bank. Take the second walled track, which heads for Coldeaton Bridge via Gipsy Bank. Pass the youth hostel. Stay on the track, which becomes more rural, for $^2/_3$ mile.

2 Climb a stile at the end of the track. Bear right, then left into the valley. Cross Coldeaton Bridge to reach the Derbyshire side of the River Dove. Turn right through a gate and follow the path downstream. Ignore a private fishing access bridge on the right. On reaching the road at Lode Mill, cross the bridge and step back into Staffordshire. Turn left along the road for Milldale.

3 Just under ½ a mile later you reach Milldale with the famous Viator's Bridge ahead of you. Keep hard right (almost doubling back) as you enter Milldale to ascend the lane past Polly's Cottage. Take care here as this can be easy to miss. This is signed 'Unsuitable for Motors' but you may get the odd bike passing you. You are climbing Millway Lane and it takes you past a Methodist chapel (built in 1835). It provides quite a testing climb initially but then levels out. The lane passes St Peter's church on your left.

4 At the main gate leading into the church bear right, back into Alstonefield to reach the George. Keep forward down the right side of the pub to return to the car park.

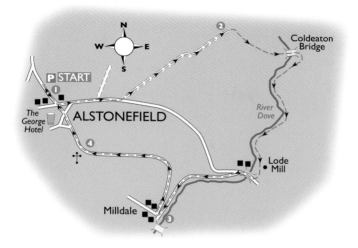

PLACES OF INTEREST NEARBY

St Peter's church in Alstonefield is worth a look while on the walk. The Cotton family pew is certainly striking, and outside there are a couple of interesting tombstones – one of which dates back to 1518 and another is in memory of someone who lived to 107 in the 18th century. Alternatively, drive down to Ilam Park (3 miles south of Alstonefield) and see stunning views of Thorpe Cloud, the famous Stepping Stones in Dovedale, limestone caves and spot the fossils at Lover's Leap. www.nationaltrust.org.uk

The stepping stones over the River Dove

20 **Thorpe**
6.8 miles (10.9 km)

WALK HIGHLIGHTS
Look out for Reynard's Cave, where a hoard of Late Iron Age and Roman coins were found in 2014. There is also a great view of Ilam Rock, made from fossilised remains around 350 million years ago.

THE PUB
The Old Dog www.theolddog.co.uk
☎ 01335 350990 **DE6 2AT**

THE WALK
1 From the car park, walk to the Old Dog. Follow the road to Thorpe to the right of it. Stay on this as it descends and bears left into the village. Take the second left (Hall Lane) towards Thorpe church.

2 Turn right at the grass triangle along Digmire Lane. Where the road bends right, follow the path in the corner. Keep forward through three fields to reach a bungalow. Keep right of this and cross the yard, passing through a gate, then another gate 15 yards later. Head through the middle of the field ahead and pass through a small gate. Descend just to the right of the buildings at the bottom of the hill.

HOW TO GET THERE: Take the A515 between Ashbourne and Buxton. At the crossroads at Tissington, turn off westwards. Just over a mile later you'll reach the Old Dog and then the Narlow Lane car park. **Postcode** DE6 2AT

MAP: OS Explorer OL24 The Peak District – White Peak area (GR 281721).

PARKING: Narlow Lane free car park or at the pub if you are a customer.

3 Turn left along the road. Immediately before the first roadbridge, turn right into the fields. Follow the path through three fields, (down the left-hand side of the first two, before heading half right in the third field) to enter woodland. The River Dove will be on your left. At the far side of the fourth field, cross the footbridge. To the left of the bridge is a café.

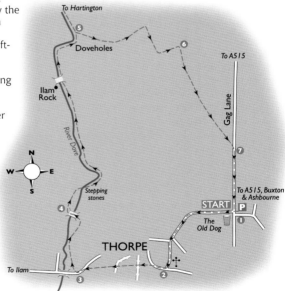

4 Turn right

along the track beyond, walking up the left side of the river to reach the stepping stones. (If they are flooded, I'm afraid there is no alternative but to retrace your steps to the start.) To continue the walk, turn left beyond the stepping stones, following the river (now on your left) for the next couple of miles. Ignore the minor paths. Look out for Reynard's Cave, above to your right. Ilam Rock is on the other side of the river. After the path bears around to the right and uphill, you reach a couple of caves known as Doveholes.

5 Some 40 yards later turn right up a narrower path, signed for Alsop-en-le-dale. A climb ensues! After a good ½ mile you come out in the open, with Hanson Grange to your left. Keep forward for 60 yards before turning right towards the walled copse of trees at the end of the field. Keep right of the copse, crossing a stile in the field corner. Keep forward over the stile into the next field with the wall on your left. In the field corner, climb a stile, turning left as you do so to walk up the left side of a wall. Cross another stile, and with the wall, then buildings, on your right, you reach a concrete drive.

6 Turn right into a farmyard, keeping all buildings on your right. At the far end, cross a stile immediately left of two farm gates. Keep alongside the wall on your right in field 1. Keep forward across field 2 and partway through field 3, bear slightly left (look out for the footpath signpost in the stone wall ahead). Keep forward in fields 4, 5 and 6 before walking down the right side of field 7. In field 8 bear slightly left, towards the stile at the bottom of the field. Bear left in field 9, cutting the corner of field 10 to reach a track. Turn left here for Gag Lane.

7 Turn right along the narrow lane. A mile later you arrive at the car park.

PLACES OF INTEREST NEARBY

Travel south to the market town of **Ashbourne**. There are many historic buildings and independent shops, and the **parish church of St Oswald's** (with a spire over 200 ft high) is worth exploring. There are also two National Trust properties in the vicinity **The Old Manor**, an early medieval hall and **Sudbury Hall and Museum of Childhood**. www.nationaltrust.co.uk